YOUR KNOWLEDGE HAS VALUE

- We will publish your bachelor's and master's thesis, essays and papers

- Your own eBook and book - sold worldwide in all relevant shops

- Earn money with each sale

Upload your text at www.GRIN.com and publish for free

Bibliographic information published by the German National Library:

The German National Library lists this publication in the National Bibliography; detailed bibliographic data are available on the Internet at http://dnb.dnb.de .

This book is copyright material and must not be copied, reproduced, transferred, distributed, leased, licensed or publicly performed or used in any way except as specifically permitted in writing by the publishers, as allowed under the terms and conditions under which it was purchased or as strictly permitted by applicable copyright law. Any unauthorized distribution or use of this text may be a direct infringement of the author s and publisher s rights and those responsible may be liable in law accordingly.

Imprint:

Copyright © 2014 GRIN Verlag
Print and binding: Books on Demand GmbH, Norderstedt Germany
ISBN: 9783668752481

This book at GRIN:

https://www.grin.com/document/433237

Katharina Gerhardt

"Everyman's" Drama with Growing Older. An Analysis of the Main Character

"My Lifestyle Determines My Death Style"

GRIN Verlag

GRIN - Your knowledge has value

Since its foundation in 1998, GRIN has specialized in publishing academic texts by students, college teachers and other academics as e-book and printed book. The website www.grin.com is an ideal platform for presenting term papers, final papers, scientific essays, dissertations and specialist books.

Visit us on the internet:

http://www.grin.com/

http://www.facebook.com/grincom

http://www.twitter.com/grin_com

Johannes Gutenberg-Universität Mainz

Fachbereich 05: Philosophie und Philologie

Summer Term 2014

Proseminar: Age & Aging in American Literature

"My Lifestyle Determines My Death Style"[a]
- Everyman's Drama with Growing Older

Katharina Gerhardt

Content

1. Introduction 3
2. Analysis 4
   2.1 Origin of Fear of Aging 4
   2.2 Lifestyle and dealing with Aging Process 5
   2.3 Consequences of Behavior 7
3. Conclusion 8
4. List of Works Cited 9

1. Introduction

"'But there's no remaking reality,' . . . . 'Just take it as it comes. Hold your ground and take it as it comes. There's no other way'" (Roth 78-79).

This quotation from *Everyman's* main character himself gives a good insight into the theme of this novel. It deals with the limitation of life which at some point becomes real for everyone, and a man's attempt to escape this reality. The book describes the hard truth that there is no turning back, once you have realized your mistakes, you will have to live with the consequences.

For most of his life though, the main character does not accept what he advices his daughter in the previous quote, namely that there is no way around reality. At some point of his life, his only aim is to escape death (71). Before that, however, he tries to elude growing older, hence starting a race against time, although he knows, he can never win.

As Robert Kastenbaum explains, "[a]nxiety- all anxiety- is rooted in the awareness of our mortality. The consequences are enormous, and reveal themselves in virtually every aspect of individual and cultural life" (137-38). The protagonist is caught up in a frantic fear of aging which is at the same time connected to a fear of loss. Therefore, he does not immediately realize the damage he has caused to others and to himself. This leads to the thesis that in Philip Roth's novel *Everyman*, the main character's destructive behavior towards relationships, mirrors his desperate attempt to cope with his own aging process.

The first chapter of this analysis will reveal the origin of the main character's fear of aging by examining the reasons and the development of his anxiety. After that chapter two will discuss these findings in relation to the protagonist's way of living and his dealing with his own aging process. In the last section the consequences of his behavior will be worked out. Furthermore, the reasons for his increasing loneliness as he grows older and his lonely death will be analyzed.

2. Analysis
2.1 Origin of Fear of Aging

The main character's fear of aging is a deep-seated anxiety, rooted in his early encounters with disease and death. The experience he makes, when he has to stay in the hospital for his hernia operation and the memory of a drowned seaman's body that had washed up on the beach, basically mark the beginning of his trauma, his frantic fear of death and ultimately also of aging: "Memorable enough that he was in the hospital that young, but even more memorable that he had registered a death. The first was the bloated body, the second was this boy" (Roth 27).

From then on, the inevitability of death starts haunting his thoughts. As Lois Tyson points out, experiences like that unconsciously influence our psyche. Therefore, it may happen that a person's childhood experiences affect his or her manner of behaving as an adult later on, as it is seen in the protagonist (12).

This trauma continues throughout his life and appears at moments when it is least expected. His fears reappear in him, for example, in the symbol of the sea, when he thinks that he has finally found stability in his life (30). The sea stands for uncontrollable vastness, comparable to the ubiquity of death and symbolizes his fear of losing the solidity of his life. His main problem seems to be that his fear of aging is connected to a fear of instability, loss, and loneliness. Tyson explains this phenomenon saying that

> [...], we will see that [...] fear of death, is intimately connected to a number of other psychological realities [...]. First and foremost, [...], the thought of our own death keys into our fear of abandonment, our fear of being alone. Death is the ultimate abandonment: no matter how close we are to our loved ones, [...], when we die, we die alone. (22)

This is all linked to the failure of his three marriages and the increasing physical decay of his body. Over the years, he needs several operations, while his older brother stays healthy. The most significant operation is the one in his left carotid artery, for which he decides to only have a local anesthetic and after which his hospitalizations become more frequent (Roth 69-71). The main character therefore cannot help envying his older brother for having everything that he had, but was never able to keep. All these things help strengthening his fears, because they are all, to some extent, connected to a feeling of losing, whether it is his health, his partner or his good relationship to his brother.

"He'd married three times, had mistresses and children and an interesting job where he'd been a success, but now eluding death seemed to have become the central business of his life and bodily decay his entire story" (71). This quote shows the contradiction in his life. He had everything, but nonetheless it never made him happy, because in the end it all comes back to his main goal, namely to escape the transience of life, and his fear of losing both his youth and his vitality.

As a consequence, the protagonists' fear of death originates in his traumatizing experiences as a child. Since he is afraid of death, he is also afraid of growing older which is accompanied by the fear of losing his ability to attract women, losing his health, and losing control over his life (Tyson 23). Ultimately, one can say that his fear of aging and death is rooted in his fear of loss and instability. Death is a loss of the self and everything familiar. As Alex Hobbs underlines in regard to the operation in which the main character remained conscious: "This sentiment represents the protagonist's approach to the ageing process as a whole: he has no control over where his body will take him and where his life will end" (12).

Of course, there are other factors that contribute to his anxiety, for instance, his lack of religiousness, because he does not know what will happen after death, but that would go beyond the scope of this analysis. In the following, *Everyman's* main character and his way of living and attempt to deal with these fears and his own aging process will be examined.

2.2 Lifestyle and dealing with Aging Process

The protagonist's attempt to cope with his aging process is mostly self-destructive. He tries to repress his fears, preserve his youth, and convince himself that his aging process is not too far advanced yet, by continuously starting new affairs. As Georgiana Banita describes in her article, sexual relations to women become a remedy for the main character, as he assigns an important role to them. They make him feel alive and, if necessary, bring him back to life, when his health issues get worse (105).

Everyman's main character keeps on running away from responsibilities and he always searches for a way to prove to himself that he has not lost his vitality yet, but rather succeeded in regaining it, as the affair with his nurse Maureen shows (Roth 50).

> Like Mickey Sabbath, the protagonist equates life with being sexually attractive to another, which includes the opportunity to be sexually active. The protagonist does not feel old because he is unable to perform sexually, but because he can no longer attract a partner. (Hobbs 15)

This demonstrates the significant role he ascribes to his affairs. These affairs are a confirmation that he has kept his youth, especially when his physical decay gets worse. As

Phoebe suggests, he is a man who cannot live without the sexual acknowledgment by other women that he is still alive, that he still has the power to attract others (Roth 122).

What he does not realize though is that he constantly distances himself from the life he actually wants to live: a balanced, stable life that does not constantly remind him of the fact that it will end some day. With his lifestyle, however, he denies his own aging process and instead of coping with death and his anxieties, he represses them and tries to prove to himself, mainly through finding out, whether women still find him sexually attractive, that he does not in fact have to "worry about oblivion", yet (32).

Once he cannot get this acknowledgment anymore, there is no way for him to assure that he has kept his youthfulness and that old age has not caught up with him, yet.

> Nothing any longer kindled his curiosity or answered his needs, not his painting, not his family, not his neighbors, nothing except the young women who jogged by him on the boardwalk in the morning. My God, he thought, the man I once was! (130)

As this text passage reveals again, the protagonist's only interest or joy is in the prospect of having another affair with a younger woman in the hope that she may restore his vitality once more. Therefore, one can say that his entire life, he runs from one relationship to the other in order to gain something that lasts and is stable, but at the same time he distances himself from all the responsibilities he has as a husband and father. Victoria Aarons suggests a contrast in Roth's protagonists as well, saying that they,

> are caught between the competing desire to depart, on the one hand from a life that no longer 'fits,' a life that seems to have worn out its possibilities, delimited by its banality, that is, psychoanalytically, by its inevitable trajectory toward death and, on the other hand, a desire to return, to hold fast to that which is familiar and safe: forward movement and retreat. (3)

So ultimately his death and aging anxiety, developed through his trauma, makes him search for stability and crave intimacy with someone, because it means to at least partly escape this feeling of total abandonment that comes with death. By trying to achieve this, however, he does not realize that he actually looks for the affection of increasingly younger women, because they give him a feeling of not getting older, while destroying the stable, lasting relationships in his life. He cannot commit himself to one person, because after a while of being with the same person, the excitement is gone and he would have to face his fears again. His fear of losing his vitality and his life, urges him to seek for the sexual acknowledgment he needs in order to repress these fears. In the next chapter of the analysis the consequences of how he tries to cope with his anxieties are examined.

2.3 Consequences of Behavior

The consequences of the main character's reactions to his aging process climax in his lonely death during his last operation. Before this, it is obvious that he already understands, he has abandoned everyone whom he meant something to, believing that he could still find what he was looking for. At the very end he learns that it was always out of reach for him, because of the way he looked for it. As a consequence, he is the one who does not have anyone to go to anymore. His second wife already told him that he would have to cope with his problems alone (Roth 122). He had robbed himself of every chance to accept his aging process and to cope with his anxieties as well as the fact that there is no alternative to death:

> Well, he was thrice divorced, a one-time serial husband distinguished no less by his devotion than by his misdeeds and mistakes, and he would have to continue to manage alone. From here on out he would have to manage everything alone. (160)

He betrayed and lied to his partners on the one hand, but wanted stability and intimacy on the other hand. As he represses his fear of death, he also stays unaware of this contradiction in his life and the fact that he tries to cover up the real meaning of his fears. *Everyman's* main character isolates and disengages himself, as he grows older, because he begins to realize that he did not only deceive others, but he mainly deceived himself. When he tries to attract another woman for the last time and fails, he starts to regret his mistakes and is forced to accept his aging process and the consequences of his former way of living (130-34).

Alex Hobbs rightly points out that all of his life the unnamed character continuously wants to replace one wife with a new and younger one, but especially as he gets older, stability becomes more essential (16). He goes on saying that although there are people who may mourn the protagonist, no one seems to be overly affected by his death (30-31).

As a conclusion, the consequence of the main character's behavior is exactly what he always feared: loss, loneliness, oblivion, passing away into nothingness without knowing it. All of this, he ends up facing on his own, because he always distanced himself from the ones who cared for him, once he found someone younger and more exciting. This can be seen clearly in the affair he has with Merete, the Danish model who becomes his third and last wife (Roth 96). He also has to accept that after Phoebe has a stroke, he cannot move in with his daughter, because her mother comes first and he finally understands that he could have the stability he needs, but he has destroyed it with his betrayal (135-139). As Debra Shostak explains, the protagonist suppresses his fears: he is obsessed with death, while at the same time he systematically avoids the prospect of its inevitability (7).

3. Conclusion

The main character's own description of his situation in the last part of this novel describes his condition very well. He had "displaced" himself, taking away every chance of coming to terms with his fears and to face the reality that awaits him (129). In the end therefore, his lifestyle indeed determines his death style, consequently turning him into a lonely, bitter, old man who has no one to go to anymore. His desperate attempt to escape the unbearable certainty of mortality and the fact that there is no way around aging turned out to be completely useless. He basically wastes his entire life going after something, not quite understanding what it really is. Only as he grows older, he begins to see that he needs stability, but he also understands that it is already too late, because as he says, "[...] decomposing families was his specialty" (158). His destructive behavior towards relationships then proved to be his way of trying, but failing to cope with his own aging process. He only pushed it all aside, repressing the reality, until it finally caught up with him so that he had to accept and also regret the failures in his life. He had to see that a person might be able to escape marriages and responsibilities throughout his or her life, but the ultimate end and the nothingness that follows are inevitable. The moment he recognized this and gave up his resistance, his life had ended.

4. List of Works Cited

Aarons, Victoria. "The Perils of Desire in Roth's Early Fiction". *CLCWeb: Comparative Literature and Culture 16.2 (2014).* Web. 14 Aug. 2014. <http://dx.doi.org/10.7771/1481-4374.2402>.

Banita, Georgiana. "Philip Roth's Fictions of Intimacy and the Aging of America".
Narratives of Life: Mediating Age. Ed. Heike Hartung and Roberta Maierhofer. Wien: LIT Verlag, 2009. 91-112. Print.

Hobbs, Alex. "A Gendered Approach to Ageing in Contemporary American Fiction: A
Portrait of the Old Man in Philip Roth's *Everyman*". *Writing into the Twenty- First Century: Essays on the American Novel.* Ed. Elizabeth Boyle and Anne-Marie Evans. Newcastle upon Tyne: Cambridge Scholars Publishing, 2010. 6-21. Print.

Kastenbaum, Robert. *The Psychology of Death.* 2nd ed. New York: Springer Publishing
Company, 1992. Print.

Metallica. "Frantic". *St. Anger.* Elektra Records, 2003. CD.[a]

Roth, Philip. *Everyman.* New York: Vintage Books, 2006. Print.

Shostak, Debra. "Roth's Graveyards, Narrative Desire, and 'Professional Competition with
Death'". *CLCWeb: Comparative Literature and Culture* 16.2 (2014). Web. 17 Aug. 2014 < http://dx.doi.org/10.7771/1481-4374.2407>.

Tyson, Lois. *Critical Theory Today: A User-friendly Guide.* 2nd ed. London: Routledge, 2007, Print.

YOUR KNOWLEDGE HAS VALUE

- We will publish your bachelor's and master's thesis, essays and papers

- Your own eBook and book - sold worldwide in all relevant shops

- Earn money with each sale

Upload your text at www.GRIN.com and publish for free